Economy is the method by which we prepare today to afford the improvements of tomorrow.
— Calvin Coolidge, 30th President of the United States of America

Table of Contents

OUR SHINING CITY

In 1776 when the United States was formed mankind reached a new height in our long climb from the swamps. America was, and is, the most perfect union ever formed by human beings. This great republic of ours truly is exceptional, and set apart from every other nation on earth. It is my fullest belief that it is America's destiny to guide mankind into the future, protected by peace through strength, and guided by the light of liberty.

Of course our nation is not perfect, nor will it ever be. And because of this obvious fact people have begun losing faith in American exceptionalism. But only because they don't understand the term. America is not better than every other country because he have the strongest military, or because we are the richest nation in history. America is better than every other country because of our unique dedication to the ideals of peace, freedom, and liberty, that you find nowhere else on earth. From its conception America was the world's greatest country, and it will continue to be the greatest country as long as we dedicate ourselves to our founding principles.

In America today we have largely lost sight of our importance, and our direction. As President Reagan said, "It is time for us to realize that we are too great a nation to limit ourselves to small dreams. We're not, as some would have us believe, doomed to an inevitable decline. I Do not believe in a fate that will fall on us no matter what we do. I do believe in a fate that will fall on us if we do nothing." It is important for us now to decide our direction, and to move towards our nation destiny. Let me share with you my vision for a beautiful shining city.

Imagine an American filled with technology but connected to its roots. A nation striving towards the future but that learns from its past. It's filled with people of every kind living in harmony, all guided by the same basic principles of freedom and justice. We prevent wars with amazing strength other countries could only dream of, and we promote the sanctity of the individual around the globe.

Imagine a America free from scarcity and want because the awesome creative power of the free market and entrepreneurial spirit have allowed us to create the systems and machines necessary to extract all the natural wealth from our land substantially. A sort of consumer agrarianism, farming for Americans in the future wouldn't be like farming today. We already possess the technology to provide food for ourselves the technology needed to transfer the production of our food from an outdoor uncertain process, to an indoor certain process. Completely free from the threat of bad weather. Mass producible and scaleable to an extent we can't imagine now. Making this transfer is to large an endeavor to be undertaken by the government, or a single individual. But the free market can, and I believe will ultimately make the transition occur at reasonable cost. After that occurs getting food will be something so simple and inexpensive that even the poorest people among us won't consider it a major expense. American future economic prosperity will be unprecedented, even in economic recessions people will enjoy more prosperity as than they do now. This will come directly from free markets and automation. Automation will drive society into a new golden age where economic growth is nearly constant. Society will of course still be ran by people, this isn't a apocalypse, but it will be ran by people using more advanced machines that ever before to accomplish their goals. These machines will do the majority of the work we do now, but quicker, more effectively, and more readily. Not to say we won't have work today. There will always be labor needed, not George Jetson"s job of pushing buttons. But meaningful work building things and designing things. There will never be massive demand for artist or poets as much as I hate to tell you. There will always be demand for welders and architects.

The tax burden will be greatly limited, government will operate on a much smaller scale, and funds will come from more voluntary sources. Americans will keep a much larger portion of their pay checks, allowing for more savings and more purchases. Houses with less tax on them than houses double their size would have currently. Bigger fancier cars, better computers and televisions, more and more luxuries. All of these products being purchased from the free market will act like fuel, giving the markets more energy to create better products and create better paying jobs. Resources to provide for this nearly constant growth will come from outer space mainly. In one asteroid there can be more iron ore than all that which has been mined on earth so far. God has given us near infinite resources in the sky, and there is nothing to stop us from making wise use of them.

Cities are massive, and integrated with aspects of wilderness as to allow people to find near spiritual escapes from the toils of everyday modern life. Man and nature work together, with man acting as a steward of the environment, conserving all our natural resources, while not being afraid to use those resources for our benefit. Everyone gets to live their lives as they see fit.

The country is strong, proud, and unafraid. The people will be freer, happier, and safer.

So how do we get there, we cut this Keynesian economics crap and let the free market operate more than we have in a very long time.

POLITICS AND COMPASSION

Politics is the most important activity of organised life in society, unfortunately. Why and in what manner people behave in their economic and political activities, should be systematically studied. That is what the study of politics seeks to do and political behaviour is almost entirely linked to economic and social behaviour and interests and vice-versa.

Nowadays young people often pompously declare: "I am not interested in politics". To them politics is some disreputable art of manipulating one's way into positions of state power for personal and party gains. And they don't look forward to being called a "politician" ever in their working lives. In fact the word has almost gradually become a term of abuse.

THE COMPASSIONATE
POLITICAL PHILOSOPHY

Libertarian conservatism is the compassionate political philosophy.

Compassion means sympathy for those who suffer, and a desire to alleviate their suffering.

Libertarians are compassionate. They understand there are moral constraints on the role of government, since government acts through force and the threat of force. When government acts beyond its limited role, it acts illegitimately and thus immorally. An immoral government cannot be a compassionate government.

Libertarians also recognize that government, as it exceeds its limited role, not only cannot act compassionately ,but also creates suffering, adds to suffering, and inhibits the alleviation of suffering. They also recognize that depending on the government to alleviate suffering limits the expression of people's natural desire to voluntarily help those in need.

GOVERNMENT CREATES SUFFERING

The government that is not limited creates suffering, because its interests conflict with citizens' interests. The natural tendency of government is to expand its size, expand its control over our lives, and expand its tax and other burdens on us. All of these are detrimental to human happiness and create suffering.

Government seeks to expand in size because it seeks to grow in power. Every new government employee means another voter dependent on the state for income. Every new program of subsidies means another industry dependent on the state for its survival. Every new program of regulation means more businesses dependent on the state for their well-being.

Government seeks to expand its scope, and thus its control over our lives, for the same reasons it seeks to expand in size: greater control means greater power. Controlled citizens are dependent on the mercy of the government. They are less likely to resist government, and more likely to capitulate to government demands.

Government seeks to expand its tax burden on us to feed its growth, to indulge its own hostility towards private wealth, and to please constituents who resent others' wealth.

Government as Parasite and Predator

Government is both parasitical and predatory. It is parasitical as it draws wealth from taxpayers, and as it commands the deployment of private resources towards its own ends. It is predatory as it endeavors to expand and monopolize the provision of services, and as it persecutes individuals and businesses for political gain.

As government pursues its own interests, it creates suffering. Its policies almost always benefit itself and its politically favored special interests rather than the public.

Its purported good intentions too often make problems worse. The bad effects are not just the products of the law of unintended consequences. They are the natural result of government's hidden intentions and recklessness.

Government cannot be honest and maintain the trust of the governed under these circumstances. Every day, we see government misrepresenting facts, misrepresenting its intentions, and misrepresenting the effects of its plans and policies.

As government does harm, its natural inclination is to make matters worse. It virtually never acknowledges its culpability in creating problems; instead, it seeks to benefit from the problems it has created. It develops new, counterproductive policies and seeks further growth.

Government also inhibits the alleviation of suffering. It acts in a self-interested, political and incompetent manner, to the detriment of the people in need. In addition, in dominating efforts, through its power and its ability to tax, it discourages people of good will from voluntarily providing help.

NEO-CONSERVATIVE AND LIBERAL PHILOSOPHIES

We have discussed the nature of government when it acts beyond its limited role, and the harm it creates. Before we discuss why libertarianism is the compassionate philosophy, let us address modern neo-national-conservative and liberal philosophies.

Neo-conservatives are not the same as classic American conservatives, the much more closely resemble European style nationalist corporatist who don't represent classical liberal beliefs common to the American right wing. To the extent there is a discernible difference in the views of neo-conservatives and liberals, it is usually just a matter of degree. Both tend to be "statists," i.e., believers in concentrating economic and political power in the central government, to the detriment of communities and individuals.

Neo-conservatives and liberals argue over the precise extent to which, or manner in which, government should be in our lives, without questioning the legitimacy of the government role in the first place. They both seek to use government to promote their own biases, as seen in the perpetual education curriculum battles, again without challenging the premise of government involvement.

Neo-National-Conservatism

Some neo-conservatives refer to themselves as "compassionate conservatives" (No this isn't a stab at President Bush, but people using that term after him). This is revealing in two ways. First, it suggests that conservatism is not inherently compassionate. Second, it implies that the liberal views the conservative is adopting are in fact compassionate.

Conservatism is inherently compassionate as it pushes for individual liberty, but modern neo-conservatism that is on the rise today is indeed not inherently compassionate, but for different reasons assumed by the self-proclaimed "compassionate conservative." It is not compassionate because it stands, just as liberalism does, for big government, with all the ills this brings upon the governed.

When neo-cons say they are compassionate, they mean in practice they think government can and should revolve around expanding centrality programs. This is a liberal idea, and it is wrong. Government can create and encourage poverty, but the only way it can reliably help the poor is to competently perform its limited role and otherwise stay out of the way.

Neo-cons claim to distinguish themselves from liberals in, among other things, their support of military action, toughness on crime, and promotion of traditional values. But they rely on the force of big government, and not on actual American principles to achieve these goals.

Liberalism

As noted, liberalism and neo-conservatism both stand for big government. They are different brands of command and control, usually with little practical difference between them.

Liberals claim the mantle of being compassionate. They claim to distinguish themselves from conservatives in areas including their support of welfare and other entitlement programs, active government involvement in personal lives from birth to death—and even after, with the estate tax, heavy regulation of business, and rescue of businesses.

But, consider examples of the consequences. Is it compassionate for government to create welfare dependency? To limit people's ability to access health care through barriers to competition? To smother business with politically motivated and often irrational regulation? To confiscate taxpayers' wealth for bailouts of politically favored entities?

Libertarianism

Libertarianism, and most importantly economic conservatism, is the compassionate political philosophy because it supports limiting the size and scope of government. It seeks to restrain government from its natural inclination to grow, to expand its control over our lives, and to take more of our resources. It thus seeks to prevent the suffering caused by unrestrained government, while restoring and preserving the freedom that exists when government is limited.

Common sense dictates skepticism towards the intent, willingness, or ability of government to act in a compassionate manner. Government acts through force or the threat of force. It appropriates its resources from the fruits of the labor, creativity, investment, and thrift of the governed.

Government's reliance on force, and its dependence on taking the wealth of others, clashes with any capacity for compassion. When government exceeds its limits, it inherently acts in an immoral manner, and cannot be considered compassionate.

Libertarians respect the natural desire of people to act in their own, voluntary ways to alleviate suffering. We believe government should stand aside in favor of the wiser, more effective efforts of individuals and private organizations.

Real compassion comes from the heart and soul, mediated by the mind. It comes from sympathy for the suffering, not from cold calculation. It leads to honest action to alleviate suffering, not taking advantage by ensnaring the sufferer or benefitting from the suffering. Hence, true compassion is best expressed freely, by free people in a free society.

Libertarianism is the compassionate political philosophy. It seeks to limit the natural tendency of government to wreak harm, while preserving the liberty of individuals to exercise true compassion.

WHAT'S WRONG WITH GOVERNMENT INTERVENTION?

Gvernment intervention in markets result in inefficiencies. Interferences make the market unfree. Of course, free markets allocate resources efficiently, so you reduce efficiency when the government interferes. You can look at all sorts of neat equilibrium models and graphs that show this to be the case.

One problem that government can introduce is the reduction of competition. Competition within markets achieves better results (economic efficiency) than when there's no or

little competition. For example, society is better off when there exist perfect competition
within a market than when there's a monopolistic firm that exerts market power. So government is decried for making markets less efficient.

ARGUMENT FOR SMALL GOVERNMENT APPROACH

Why favor smaller, less-powerful government?

So people you can't stand whose values you detest will have less power to impose their silly opinions on you.

Take your pick from these two perspectives from Don Boudreaux in his post Laissez Faire at Cafe Hayek.

If your opinions run to the left side of the political spectrum, consider this:

If you are a modern "Progressive" and cannot abide the notion of conservatives, Christian or otherwise, having a say in who you may marry, what sorts of scientific research and artistic projects should be funded, what school curricula should and shouldn't include, or when and why Uncle Sam goes on world-policing ventures, then why do you wish to expand the scope of government authority? Doing so in a society with a wide franchise, such as the U.S., inevitably invites those people you consider to be rubes to intrude what you believe to be their antediluvian superstitions and dogmas onto you and onto all that you hold dear and sacred.

If your opinions run to the right side of the political spectrum, consider this:

If you are a modern conservative, Christian or otherwise, and cannot abide the notion of "Progressives" having a say in how you school your children, what your tax rates are, what size Big Gulps you may buy, or whether or not you may fill in ditches and water puddles on your land, then why do you tolerate – or even applaud – activities such as government tariffs on imports? Doing so – by creating a large and discretionary state – only encourages those obnoxious know-it-alls to use government against you and against all that you hold dear and sacred.

I can see the reactions to those two paragraphs. I bet everyone looks at the first half of one paragraph and says "yeah! Right!" and looks at the first half of the other saying "wait a second, that's over the top hyperbole!" Only difference will be which paragraph you think is a factually accurate description of reality and which is silly exaggeration.

It doesn't matter which party holds the White House, Senate, and House today or in 8 years or even 16 years from now. More powerful, intrusive government, with increasing amounts of money to spend, and unrestrained authority to write new regulations will either now or later allow people whose values you vigorously disagree with to make decisions on how you live your life.

1. How to get less of whatever you detest?

Simple,

Less powerful, less intrusive government with less regulatory authority over your every breath.

Doesn't matter which side of any issue you stand and whether you look at the House or Senate. Eventually, the other side will have power.

2. Reason of Argument

This is a Universal Truth, Inspiring and Amazing in its magnitude :

"Human beings control their destiny! They possess the power to create the life they want and stretch beyond their wildest imaginations to make their most astonishing and impossible dreams come true!

Humans are the most amazing of God's creations and have the power to reach the heavens !"

Whatever others may say about not being responsible for something that happened to them or being accountable for some venture, it was their creation and their doing!

This is our life, a precious gift - the most precious you can ever get!

We have the power and potential to rise to the stature and status of the gods (little "g", it makes a world of difference) and even surpass them!

3. Small Government Approach makes the economy better

The term "big government" stimulates plenty of images and emotions, and they're generally negative. Words like "bureaucratic," "inefficient," "intrusive," and even "corrupt" are often associated with the term. Economists charge that big government interferes with the mechanisms of free enterprise. Libertarians believe it seeks to control private or personal freedoms guaranteed by the "natural law" eloquently philosophized by John Locke and formalized in the U.S. Constitution's Bill of Rights. And politicians claim big government lacks checks and balances on its exercise of power, leading it to represent special interests to the detriment of its citizens.

Small government, on the other hand, is generally believed to lead to a more efficient and flexible system. "Getting government off our backs" or "getting government out of the way" are cries to return to the low-tax, no-regulation beliefs of the American Revolutionary period. The size of government envisioned by the country's founders sought to cast off tyranny and empower small businessmen and entrepreneurs.

Small government was best summarized by the principal author of the Declaration of Independence and third President of the United States

Thomas Jefferson when he claimed, "That government is best which governs least, because its people discipline themselves." Meg Whitman, former CEO of eBay, current CEO of Hewlett-Packard, and one-time Republican candidate for Governor of California described it as "making a small number of rules and getting out of the way. Keeping taxes low. Creating an environment for small businesses to grow and thrive."

THE PRESENT ECONOMY
OF AMERICA

A robust US economy means companies expand which results in job creation. Currently, the American people are not spending as a result of the Great Recession that just recently ended. Fortunately the current unemployment rate stands at 4.7% as of December 2016, however this may not be completely accurate due to many people dropping out of the work force previous to recovery. The recovery from the Great Recession was the slowest in American history, and the economy still isn't booming because of a decrease in spending by the American people which results in a decrease in company profits, company non-expansion, and more layoffs.

So how can the US economy improve?

STEPS TO ECONOMIC IMPROVEMENT:

The first step is to realize that it is business and not government that creates jobs and wealth within the American society.

Looking At The Brighter Side, It Is Not Yet The End Of The World (probably).

These things happen for a reason. Major causes of the initial subprime mortgage crisis and following recession include: International trade imbalances and lax lending standards contributing to high levels of developed country household debt and real-estate bubblesthat have since burst;

U.S. government housing policies. Once the recession began, various responses were attempted, these included fiscal policies of governments; monetary policies of central banks; measures designed to help indebted consumers refinance their mortgage debt; and inconsistent approaches used by nations to bail out troubled banking industries and private bondholders, assuming private debt burdens or socializing losses. The government response dragged the recession on and on. The economy barely grew under Presidents Obama because his economic policies were remarkably pro big government and bad for the economy. It's time America to stand up and to do something about this adversity. And the best thing to do about this, is what you would do anyway. Work for income, and sell stuff. As the President Calvin Coolidge said "After all, the chief business of the American people is business. They are profoundly concerned with producing, buying, selling, investing and prospering in the world." Commerce is virtuous, and the only way to insure prosperity.

HOW THE GOVERNMENT IS TAKING OVER THE ECONOMY

The market crash of 2008 destroyed many Corporations that were in fact the favored engines of "free market" growth, as governments passed on the responsibility of the economy to these giant companies. Their failure, simply meant Governments again had to step in and "save" them, leading to a de-facto Government ownership of the economy.

Most experts agree that we no longer live in a corporate-based economy, were giant corporations favored by our governments ran the economy, whilst our elected governments managed our money. This is due to the rescue of many toxic, and failed giants like our banks.

In the USA alone after a range of bailouts, stimulus packages and takeovers, an estimated 58% of Americans are dependent in some way on the US government for their income. In Europe, this percentage is much higher, especially in countries in France and Germany.

In theory we are the government, after all we elect the representatives who decide how our countries are run, whilst our taxes are for the services our government offers, and the base salaries of our elected officials. However in practice, often many of us feel, we are separated from the government, and have no real influence on how our governments are run.

The New Economy that has grown out of the market crash of 2008, illustrates this point. As State and National Governments now technically, own many of our homes and banks, after bailing out them out. In reality, this crash created a move towards a government- based economy.

An economy were we pay and elect who represents and works for us, but at the same time are dependent on ensuring our own mortgages, business loans and debts are paid to keep these governments running.

And this trend is not going to change unless we make it change . By 2015, some economists agree that the USA, the once Father of Free Market capitalism, may directly or indirectly have 67% of Americans dependent on them for their incomes. In Europe the scenario is far worse.

How does this change affect us?

Small business owners may become ever more dependent on Government sponsored grants, and tax breaks to survive. Banks will have to become more rational, and hardball about who they loan to. Governments already saddled with huge debts, may pass them on in increasing taxes, and exchanging international debts for trade.

Mortgages in effect become "de-facto" rent-buy housing from our Governments, who collect the monthly payments through the Banks they bailed out.

Businesses will become dependent on grants and stimuli packages to survive. As governments fighting the scourge of unemployment encourage business start-ups by offering financial help. Once example of this can be seen in Europe:

The European Union award grants to new businesses, often in the guise of a basic monthly wage to allow the business to run, until profits allow the business to become independent. Often this "grant" is for two years.

A good idea, right?

In most cases, after the two year period, these new businesses close their doors for good. One example was a Spanish town were the town center was turned into a scenic shopping area. After two years this area became a ghost town, as small businesses closed, once the grant ran out. These businesses became over-dependent on the European Union to finance them, and could not exist without this grant.

Dependency on large favored corporate giants caused the current effects on our economy, but a State dependent economy is definitely not a solution. A more flexible way to run an economy is needed, thankfully that more flexible way exists through the free market.

WHAT IS THE 'FREE MARKET'

The free market is a summary description of all voluntary exchanges that take place in a given economic environment. Free markets are characterized by a spontaneous and decentralized order of arrangements through which individuals make economic decisions. Based on its political and legal rules, a country's free market economy may range between very large or entirely black market.

BREAKING DOWN 'Free Market'

The term "free market" is a synonym for laissez-faire capitalism. When most people discuss the "free market," they mean an economy with unobstructed competition and only private transactions between buyers and sellers. However, a more inclusive definition should include any voluntary economic activity so long as it is not controlled by coercive central authorities.

Using this description, laissez-faire capitalism is free market economics but voluntary socialism is still not an example of a free market, because the latter includes centralized ownership of the means of production. The critical feature is the absence of coercive impositions or restrictions regarding economic activity. Coercion cannot take place in a free market even if mutually agreed to in a voluntary contract.

Connection With Capitalism and Individual Liberty

The least restrictive markets tend to coincide with countries that value private property, capitalism and individual rights. This makes sense since political systems that shy away from regulations or subsidies for individual behavior necessarily interfere less with voluntary economic transactions. Additionally, free markets are more likely to grow and thrive in a system where property rights are well protected and capitalists have an incentive to pursue profits.

Free Markets and Financial Markets

In free markets, a financial market develops to facilitate financing needs for those who cannot or do not want to self-finance. For example, some individuals or businesses specialize in acquiring savings by consistently not consuming all of their present wealth. Others specialize in deploying savings in pursuit of entrepreneurial activity, such as starting or expanding a business. These actors can benefit from trading financial securities.

For example, savers can purchase bonds and trade their present savings to entrepreneurs for the promise of future savings plus remuneration, or interest. With stocks, savings are traded for an ownership claim on future earnings. There are no modern examples of purely free financial markets.

Common Constraints on the Free Market

All constraints on the free market use implicit or explicit threats of force. Common examples include: prohibition of specific exchanges, taxation, regulations, mandates on specific terms within an exchange, licensing requirements, fixed exchange rates, competition from publicly provided services, price controls and quotas on production, purchases of goods or employee hiring practices.

Even when free market behavior is regulated, voluntary exchanges may still take place in spite of government prohibitions. Such exchanges take place in the so-called "black market," which may be considered an underground version of the free market. Competition is difficult and the price system is much less effective in a black market, so monopolistic or oligopolistic behavior is likely.

The biggest threat, as he sees it, is not the rise of China's authoritarian system of state capitalism, but the pervasive ignorance-inspired delusion among Americans that the free market is not the only driver of prosperity. This dangerous perception is on full display with the successful fear-mongering dominating the health care debate.

CRITICISM OF FREE MARKET ECONOMICS

Free market economics believes government intervention should be limited to the protection of private property. It is advocated by many economists especially in the Chicago, and Austrian school of Economics.

However, although free markets have advantages, such as greater efficiency, there are several criticisms levelled at purely free market economies.

Critiisms of free market economics

Inequality. The wealthy will tend to be able to accumulate greater wealth in a free market. This is due to:

The ability to inherit wealth

Wealthy can pay for better education for their children, giving certain groups of people a better start in life.

People with wealth and assets can use profit and dividend to purchase more assets. The rich can accumulate more.

The wealthy are likely to be able to create monopoly power, which exacerbates inequality.

In a free market, there will be periods of unemployment, leaving some people with no income.

Monopoly power. In a free market, firms with a high market share will be able to set higher prices to consumers

Under-provision of public goods (e.g. defence and law and order – goods which are non-rivalry and non-excludable)

Under-provision of merit goods like health and education – goods with positive externalities and services where people may under-estimate benefits of a good.

Information failure – a lack of information about the best way to use resources, e.g. moral hazard in insurance.

Private sector more inefficient in providing public services like health care. e.g. US pays high admin costs for private health insurance.

Instability of free markets. John Maynard Keynes argued capitalism has a tendency to boom and bust economic cycles – which leads to periods of mass unemployment. Hyman Minksy suggested that financial markets were inherently unstable due to forces of irrational exuberance. See: Financial instability.

Over-production of negative externalities e.g. environmental pollution and congestion, which lower living standards.

Over-consumption of demerit goods – goods where people may ignore or under-estimate costs, e.g. smoking, alcohol.

Unsustainability. Free markets are concerned with the present moment but ignore implications for long-term ecological stability.

For example, free markets may lead to the over-use of raw materials and

Economists critical of free market economics

Karl Marx – Marxist critique of exploitation of labour by capitalists.

John Maynard Keynes – Keynes was critical of laissez-faire with regard to boom and bust cycles.

John Atkinson Hobson – English economist supported social democracy and redistribution of income, an early critic of neo-classical views.

Henry George (1839 – 1897) – American political economist popularised criticism of free-markets in Gilded Age. His Progress and Poverty (1879) investigated inequality and advocated land-tax and redistribution of wealth.

Joseph Stiglitz – Critical of unregulated free-markets and consumer led booms. In particular, he criticises the "market fundamentalism." of Thatcher and Reagan years which assumes free markets are always the best solution.

John Kenneth Galbraith

Thomas Piketty – Capital in the Twenty-First Century Piketty's premise is that wealth grows faster than economic output, thus concentrating capital (and the income it produces) in ever-fewer hands

Kenneth Arrow – critical of the idea that free markets can solve the problem of health care. See: Uncertainty and welfare economics of health care

Paul Krugman – Critical of 'market fundamentalism'. Agrees with Arrow about limitations of free markets in areas such as health care. see: Why markets can't cure health care

These criticisms don't take into account economics or human nature.

To address probably the biggest criticism we face today, that the free market "can't cure healthcare", Quick Note on Healthcare,

Healthcare is one of the biggest problems in America, not because the free market can't control the healthcare industry, but because the government can't but believes it can. I don't know about you but I'm sick of hearing about healthcare. The affordable healthcare act (Obamacare) was a disgrace, and the republican plan to replace it is just as bad. So I'm going to let in you on a little secret, healthcare isn't hard to fix. The reason why it hasn't been fixed is because democrats have this Delusional idea that Europe style socialized healthcare is a utopian dream (it actually sucks), so they forced it down the throats of unwilling Americans. The health care cost crisis didn't begin until the government got involved by creating Medicare and Medicaid, because when you artificially stimulate demand, there's no incentive to lower prices, then when republicans moved into a position to repeal it they scared everyone they possiblycould by telling them they would literally die if republicans got rid of Obamacare. Multiple studies have found that Obamacare hasn't saved a single life, but in fact cost Americans tons of money and has potentially ruined the American healthcare industry for decades to come. However, because of all the hyperbole republicans are now afraid that if they repeal Obamacare the scared masses will throw them out of office, to try to compensate they want to make a plan to "repeal and replace" so people feel safe and vote for them again. This won't help because what the healthcare industry actually needs is to be treated like an industry again. The best way to lower the price of healthcare is to have hospitals and health insurances competing for your business against each other. That way only the companies that can provide quality service at the lowest possible prices will continue to not go bankrupt while the ones that do cost too much do go bankrupt and are pushed out of the market. I am not an evolutionist, but in the competitive market Darwinian processes do apply.

But the government thinks it can help, the government tried this same stunt with auto manufacturers when it looked like foreign cars might over take American production. The auto industry became dependent on government money to exist, then became uncompetitive, people bought the better (foreign) cars, the government money dried up. Fast forward to today and not a single car in produced solely in America now. The auto industry is building back up, but after the government gets involved it's hard to recover. Just like President Ronald Reagan said," The most terrifying words in the English language are: I'm from the government and I'm here to help."

WHY FREE-MARKET ECONOMICS
WORK BEAUTIFULLY

If there's one thing everyone in Americas should know, it's that true and free markets are best.

After all, we're not Communists, as much as some angsty teens may want us to be. The communist starved and lost the Cold War because they believed in stupid ideas. And their watered-down European cousins, the socialists? More of the same, only less so. Europe is facing a massive economic crisis as a direct result of their big government centralized economics.

Here's why that doesn't work: a truly free market is a perfectly competitive market. Which means that whatever you have to sell in that market, so does your competition. Which means price war. Which means your price gets driven down. Which means products are cheap and easily accessible for consumers .

Naturally, businesses still want to make as big profits as possible, so they try to make their products seem better than their competitors so they can marginally raise prices. In fact, the fine art of doing so is a big part of what they teach in business schools.

That's why businesses use strategies like product differentiation, so their competition is no longer selling the exact same product they are. That's why they use strategies like branding, so the products are the same, so they keep innovating and improving to stay alive as a business.

They don't improve their products and services because the government is making them somehow, they do it because they have an intrinsic economic incentive to. Always.

This is part of the innate essence of capitalism.. It is part of what makes the whole system go. It is part of what makes capitalism capitalism.

People are the same way. Consider your own career. Why do you get paid more than the minimum wage? (I'm hoping you do.) Probably because you have some skill that everybody else doesn't have. So you don't have to bid against every unemployed person in your area to hold your job. Just a few of them. Which pushes your wage above the legal minimum (even though minimum wage hurts all workers.

That skill of yours is what economists call a "barrier to entry" — entry into the market for your job, that is.

Now let's consider the other side of the equation. We've looked at free markets in things you sell. Now let's consider free markets in things you buy.

THE BRILLIANCE OF FREE MARKETS TO SOLVE PROBLEMS

we live in a country that is known for free-market capitalism, that has also been known to solve every problem it has ever been presented. Let me give you a for instance.

The academics and political class want us to stop using oil and fossil fuels. They tell us that we should use battery-powered cars, and generate our electricity using renewable energy, and alternative energy strategies. No mind that may not actually work, but let's go ahead and proceed with this line of thinking. Next, they run into a problem where there is not another lithium on the open market to supply all the batterie ?

Worse, most of the lithium mines in the United States have been shut down, and the big reserves are in countries like China and Bolivia. Both of them would like to hold that lithium for ransom to make those ion-lithium batteries, and become in essence the new OPEC. Since the intellectually self-proclaimed powers that be can't get very much lithium, they have to make the batteries smaller, that means the range of the cars won't be as far, so they have to make highbred autos instead, cars which also have a small motor that can run the car after it runs out of juice.

Then they decided they we need to be able to charge the batteries faster, and so they make mandates that gas stations also have rapid charging system available for electric cars so the motorist won't get stranded. This will ensure that more motorists will buy electric cars, because they will save money, get tax incentives, and the government will subsidize the energy production as long as it's from alternative clean energy.

Still, if there is a real problem in the world we should let free enterprise solve it, because that's what they're good at. If someone is willing to spend the money to get their car rapidly charged, entrepreneurs will find a way to fill that need as long as they make money. It turns out that Cracker Barrel will install electric car charging stations in its parking lots. No offense to the competition but this is absolutely brilliant. You see, if you are traveling down the freeway, and you're getting low on juice in your electric car, you can stop in for lunch or dinner at Cracker Barrel, and charge it up there.

The restaurant will get more patrons, they will solve the problem of the motorists, and we didn't really need government intervention for any of it did we, motorists can still take long trips in electric cars now? I wish the politicians and academics would understand that the entrepreneurs are a lot smarter than they give them credit for. I would submit to you that if the politicians and academics were smart as us, they would be making a whole lot more money out here in the real world and be solving a lot more problems, rather than trying to make our lives tough. Indeed I hope you will please consider all this and think on it.

MORE FREE MARKETS

In a free market economy, the law of supply and demand, rather than a central government, regulates production and labor. Companies sell goods and services at the highest price consumers are willing to pay, while workers demand the highest wages companies are willing to pay for their services. A purely capitalist economy is a free market economy; the profit motive drives all commerce and forces businesses to operate as efficiently as possible to avoid losing market share to competitors.

Command economies are marked by communist and socialist tendencies. The government controls the means of production and the distribution of wealth, dictating the prices of goods and services, and the wages workers receive.

Free market economies and command economies exist more as abstract concepts than as tangible realities; almost all of the world's economies feature elements of both systems. For example, while the U.S. allows companies to set prices, and workers negotiate wages, the government establishes parameters, such as minimum wages and antitrust laws, that must be followed. Antitrust laws work to compliment the free market, they prevent the formation of private monopolies keeping the market competitive. The minimum wage however harms the market, and individuals by taking competitiveness out of the labor market, and giving big companies like Walmart loopholes to work with to pay employees less than if the minimum wage didn't exist. Not to mention the pressure it places on businesses to phase out all labor for automation instead. Although you could argue that's a natural process in an industrialized economy, it still prevents workers from adapting to new positions in place of the old.

TAXATION AND THE GOVERNMENT

History Of Tax

It's hard to determine when taxes first were levied to citizens of an established country. Rulers had always collected from subservient subjects. The first taxes were tribute paid to warlords for protection, although this concept most likely dates back to the first time someone was stronger than other people and decided they deserved things because of that.

China and Egypt

Ancient China subscribed to various forms of taxation that might be considered income tax, and Egyptian Pharaohs placed taxation on their people, too. Those who collected taxes for the Pharaoh were called scribes, and one way that the Monarchs made sure they received tax was by placing it on cooking oil. The scribes would go into homes and do inspections to determine that everyone was using enough cooking oil.

Modern Taxation

Throughout history, every organized society had some form of government. In free societies, the goals of government have been to protect individual freedoms and to promote the well-being of society as a whole.

To meet their expenses, the government "need" income, which it raises through taxes. In our country, governments levy several different types of taxes on individuals and businesses.

The Federal Government relies mainly on income taxes for its revenue. State governments depend on both income and sales taxes. Most county and city governments use property taxes to raise their revenue. All of this takes money out of your hands, and limits what you are able to do. Therefore it should be a goal to limit taxes to the bare minimal

Taxes In The United States

Governments pay for these services through revenue obtained by taxing three economic bases: income, consumption, and wealth. The Federal Government taxes income as its main source of revenue. State governments use taxes on income and consumption, while local governments rely almost entirely on taxing property and wealth.

Taxes On Income

The earnings of both individuals and corporations are subject to income taxes. Most of the Federal Government's revenue comes from income taxes. The personal income tax produces about five times as much revenue as the corporate income tax.

Not all income tax taxed in the same way. For example, taxpayers owning stock in a corporation and then selling it at a gain or loss must report it on a special schedule. This

item and any other gains or losses get calculated separately before they get added to other income. By comparison, the interest they earn on money in a regular savings account gets included with wages, salaries, and other "ordinary" income. There are also many types of tax-exempt and tax-deferred savings plans available that impact on people's taxes.

Payroll taxes are a major source of revenue for the Federal Government. Employers are responsible for paying these taxes, which include social security insurance and unemployment compensation. Employees also pay into the social security program through money withheld from their paychecks. Some state governments also use payroll taxes to pay for the state's unemployment compensation programs.

Over the years, the amount paid in social security taxes has greatly increased. This is because fewer workers are paying into the system for each retired person now receiving benefits. Today, some workers pay more social security tax than income tax.

Taxes On Consumption

The most important taxes on consumption are sales and excise taxes. Sales taxes usually get paid on such things as cars, clothing and movie tickets. Sales taxes are a major source of revenue for most states and some large cities and counties. The tax rate varies from state to state, and the list of taxable goods or services also varies from one state to the next.

Excise taxes, sometimes called "luxury taxes," are used by both state and Federal Governments. Examples of items subject to Federal excise taxes are heavy tires, fishing equipment, airplane tickets, gasoline, beer and liquor, firearms, and cigarettes.

The objective of excise taxation is to place the burden of paying the tax on the consumer. A good example of this use of excise taxes is the gasoline excise tax. Governments use the revenue from this tax to build and maintain highways, bridges, and mass transit systems. Only people who purchase gasoline -- who use the highways -- pay the tax.

Some items get taxed to discourage their use. This applies to excise taxes on alcohol and tobacco. Excise taxes are also used during a war or national emergency. By raising the cost of scarce items, the government can reduce the demand for these items.

Taxes On Property And Wealth

The property tax is local government's main source of revenue. Most localities tax private homes, land, and business property based on the property's value. Usually, the taxes get paid monthly along with the mortgage payment. The one who holds the mortgage, such as a bank, holds the money in an "escrow" account. Payments then get made for the property owner.

Some state and local governments also impose taxes on the value of certain types of "personal" property. Examples of personal property often taxed are cars, boats, recreational vehicles, and livestock.

Property taxes account for more than three-fourths of the revenue raised through taxes on wealth. Other taxes imposed on wealth include inheritance, estate, and gift taxes.

TAX BRACKETS

The tax system is a key tool for redistributing wealth, which in the long run hurts the economy and every American. Some gap between rich and poor is critical to maintaining a healthy balance to a market-based economy. The goal shouldn't be to level incomes so to cap maximum income, but to try to raise all incomes by allowing the market system to work. People like Bill Gates will always exist, and will always be drastically richer than the average person. It doesn't help anyone to cut them down to size. In fact Bill Gates' wealth helps everyone by allowing him to run Microsoft, thereby creating goods and services that we want or depend on for our businesses and professional life's, therefore allowing us to make more money or be more productive. Not to mention the immediate benefit of all the employees Bill Gates can pay the salaries of by having so much wealth. The free market works very well because it receives signals on what should be produced from demand by the members of society because of their desire to ensure that their basic needs are met. If taxes prevent businesses from creating products cheaply then there will be disastrous consequences in terms of jobs and economic growth.

Social and economic disparities brought on by the government trying to redistribute threatens the republic itself as those in positions of power influence political decision-making not based off of sound political theory, but for virtue signaling to their base, and do so to protect and strengthen their own interests. A flat tax system focused on funding more of the government through voluntary avenues will help to increase the prosperity of all Americans by boosting the economy because such a plan would stimulate consumer spending by middle and lower income Citizens. Lower tax rates on all income brackets should be restored. The best way to help Americans through taxes is simple, instead of raising taxes on the rich to where they move their assets out of the country, causing everyone to suffer, we should lower taxes on everyone, so everyone can Benefit . If we cut taxes on the wealthy by 40%, then those top income earners would have 40% more income to spend on expanding businesses, hiring new employees, and creating new products. Then if we also lowed taxes by 40% on middle class Americans, and say 40% on low income Americans, then they would have 40%

more income to buy things with or to save. They could buy better cars, repair or remodel their homes. This increase in consumer buying would act to turbo charge our economy. The money spent would go to business to invest in expanding, hiring more people, creating new products. As labor became in more demand wages go up organically without destructive government interference. As wages go up people have more money to spend on products, the cycle continues.

The lesson is clear: Low tax rates lift up the lives of America's poor.

Though this seems rather clear many people argue that government can reduce poverty by "redistributing" wealth through progressive taxation – imposing higher tax rates on higher income brackets – and through more government spending. This is utter nonsense, when a state has a low tax burden, economic growth is stronger. Economic growth delivers more job creation and higher per capita and median family incomes. Low tax rates lift up the lives of Economic growth is a powerful means to pull people out of poverty.

Although some policymakers justify high taxes for the sake of the poor, the data show that higher taxes and related spending do little to reduce poverty rates. Rather, states with healthy economic climates have much more success in lifting people out of poverty.

The causes of and solutions to, poverty is complex, but one policy is clear: Low tax rates are a significant factor in achieving the universal goal of poverty reduction.

AMERICA, HECK YEAH

To move from America to any other nation in the world, we have to give up an awful lot. We'd have to begin with our automobiles because no other country enjoys the individual freedom of travel we have here. We'd have to give up over half our cars to compete with most nations. This wouldn't seem too bad, though, because we'd also have to give up about two-thirds of our streets and highways too - just to compete with other nations.

America only has about 6% of the world's population, and only occupies about 7% of the world's land surface, yet we have about 75% of the world's appliances, televisions, and other conveniences. One luxury we have, that many people in other parts of the world don't have, is the luxury of moving our residences. It is estimated the average America family moves about every seven years. In many parts of the world, two or three families share what we would call a single family residence.

We enjoy freedom in this country that isn't even understood by other people. We have a free enterprise system second to none in the world. In other nations, it's often pre- determined even where a person will work, and many other things that affect them. In America, we tend to take for granted things that don't even exist in other parts of the world. And have you traveled recently, and have you looked for various choices in the supermarkets of other nations? The choices they have - if any - are extremely limited. We walk into the store and have ten choices of anything we want. I remember a story of two Brits in London one day ordering ice cream. One said to the other: "I can't believe those bloody Americans with 32 choices of ice cream. I can hardly decide between chocolate and vanilla."

Our nation truly is a land of pride and plenty.

Of course, we have our problems. Just less than every other country.